She Is Made Of Chalk

By L. M. Dorsey

Dedication

I'd be a fool to not dedicate this book to the two things that were the driving forces behind my writing anything, Fear and Love.

The biggest 'Thank You' to my Editor and all around dynamic person Joanne, also thanks for the title inspiration.

Thank you to my family for infinite support. I love you all dearly.

Hopefully this is just the beginning!

Russian Roulette

   they say
that she just likes to fight

but she's made of chalk
   writing stories
with each one
of her broken parts

her allure was ample
   at first glance
a second before
he was lost to her charms

as she played Russian roulette
  with her heart
just another bullet
in the chamber

click, click, click
& she shoots to kill.

-Joanne Hammadi

Prologue

I am guilty of not seeing myself clearly. It's not really a crime and we all are guilty of it, so I try not to hold it against myself, but I do. Even now as I stand in front of the mirror picking apart the flaws in my face I am not seeing me. To be completely forthcoming I haven't the slightest clue who the fuck I am. I do things, I love things, I love people, but this girl whose lips move when I want to say something, I have no idea who she is.

Maybe that is what I most guilty of, not knowing myself. I think that very reason is why I have been itching to write something about me. I have started so many times but I never know where to start. I tried writing about this guy I liked but I felt really self-conscious about it. I still have it and maybe I will include part of it in this, whatever this thing is I am writing but for now, I guess I am on the road to self discovery.

I actually hate that turn of phrase - self discovery - I am going to rephrase it, I am embarking on a path of self -

revelation. I like that. It sounds better, sounds more spiritual and less selfish. Although having revelations of one's self can be seen as somewhat selfish. That's really not much my concern even though I keep talking about it. Moving on.

I was going to back track and try and give you a back story to how my life began from humble beginnings and blah, blah, blah but I am not. I am going to jump right into now because now is where I need the help. Now is where I am fucked. Now is where I am. The past is always around, I guess it will revel it's self in due time... see revelation.

I had a thought today as I was sitting on my stepmother's evergreen, worn to perfection, leather couch. *What would it be like to be dead?* Don't worry I am not suicidal and the thought didn't come out of nowhere. I was looking at a picture of my Aunt who pasted away in January '09. I was thinking she is like a whisper. She quietly hangs over every part of my life. It's weird, a little depressing at times, but I can feel her presence softly nudging me to have an experience. Not just be alive, as I have been. Move past my fears or anything that is holding me back in anyway from being free and loving the life I have.

I don't much care for being dead yet and I would love to love and be free, so I'll take this step in good faith and begin

down the path to revelation with you all
looking over my shaky unsure shoulders.
Let the journey begin.

Sometimes,
I feel like
the only part of me
that is accessible
 is sadness.

Hollow

I am standing under the rain fall of my shower head. The moist droplets beat music into my back. Echo through to my ribs and vibrate through my chest. I watch as runaway beads of water snake down my breasts.

Then I think, *I can't be this hollow.* My heart can't be this silent. The thick layers of skin, muscle and fatty tissue should have absorbed the vibration, should have muddled the percussion of my drum tight back. I should have never seen the waters rhythm dance across my chest like crumbs bouncing around on an exposed speaker. I think, *I can't be this hollow.* What scares me is the thought, *I just might be.*

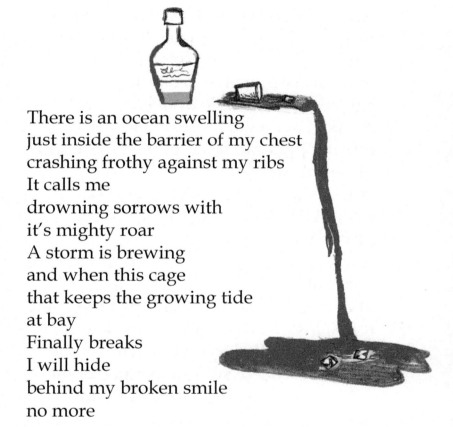

There is an ocean swelling
just inside the barrier of my chest
crashing frothy against my ribs
It calls me
drowning sorrows with
it's mighty roar
A storm is brewing
and when this cage
that keeps the growing tide
at bay
Finally breaks
I will hide
behind my broken smile
no more

I Am Not Whole

I am not whole.
And toting this notion over my head that
people should not be broken or some how
after you have been broken you can be
fixed, pieced together, collected shards,
jigsaw puzzle people fitting together
perfectly with no noticeable seams, no
missing pieces to be accounted for. I find it
incredible miraculous that no one speaks
of the pieces that get lost, those holes that
can not be filled within us. The dark
places in our lives.

I am not whole.
I have been broken and chipped too many
times, lost too many shards while tidying
up, accidentally kicked too many pieces
under the couch, swept too much of the
debris under the rug to ever account
myself as whole. I don't even know what's
missing. I can't say I miss the forgotten

pieces. Those phantom limbs are still there somewhere. I am almost certain of it.

I am not whole.
I have given too much of myself away.
Cut it out of my chest and planted a white flag in it. It is yours, you can have, I said as I surrendered. I feel for it everyday. I pat hopelessly at air hoping its back there but its not. I check the box I collect my broken pieces in over and over hoping it's all there. It's not.

I don't like this feeling, this not feeling whole.

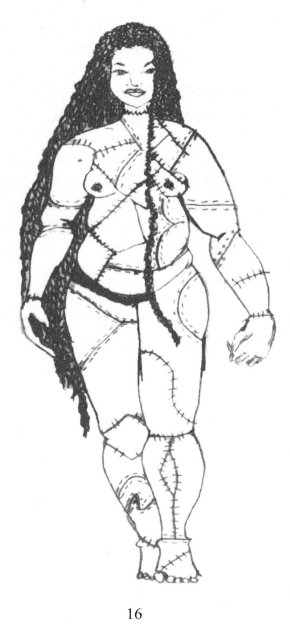

16

Thank You Grandma Lynch, Because I Forgot To

I was eighteen years old before anybody had ever told me that I was beautiful. Yeah, sure, when I was little I was cute and pretty and all the other things you tell a little girl to abate her lack of self-esteem. Those are things no one ever has to mean, you can just say them without thought. You can just say your beautiful too, but the fact that it is never done proves the phase holds much more weight. Thus, the fact of my being beautiful never graced its way across anyone's lips. I didn't know I should hear it either. I spent my high school years battling post traumatic stress, with no one to help me and no where to voice my pain but my journal. Everyone around me went on with their lives while I suffered in silence so long that I wanted to die. Everyday I prayed for death and every night I cried, sobbing deep down to my soul, wondering what was wrong with me. So, I never even thought I need to hear I was beautiful, so many other things were more important to me than that at the time.

But it was there waiting for me, crammed in with the suffocating Texas heat and the possibility of fashion design as a major in college in my eighteenth year summer vacation. It was given by a little old lady with failing health and gnarled hands, my great grandmother. I can't say I would have remembered it if everyone fawned over me daily and threw themselves at my feet, or erected statues in my likeness confessing my beauty. But, I did remember it because that was the first time I had heard it, ever. And it was given during a time I really needed to hear it. I was drowning under a hideously unsolved sexual assault, -I, nor my family had gotten any help to deal with it- I was not sleeping, I couldn't focus, I was scared all the time (sometimes, most times I still am), which kept my stomach in knots and me constantly vomiting. I needed a hand

up or a way out. It had been to long
suffering, I couldn't take it anymore. I was
done struggling just to leave the house
every morning. I had declared it, sitting in
my grandmother's house watching TV,
avoiding conversation with my great
grandmother whom sat across from me.

From the outside it looked like an
ordinary summer vacation for any
recently graduate high school student,
visiting family members before their first
semester of college. And it was. The TV
was blaring Days of Our Lives because
that is what my great grandmother
watched, her soaps. I was sewing
something by hand, trying to

disappearing in to the crushed blue velvet of the sofa, wanting so badly to just become another room accessory. Then out of nowhere she spoke in her clear voice that always signified authority. I always pictured her moving mountains with her voice that was so low but strong.

"You know Kecia, you are really beautiful." My grandmother professed her statement like she had just discovered that I was in the room with her.

"Thanks grandma," I smiled briefly before cutting my eyes back to the project that sat in my lap.

But she wouldn't let it go. She sat up straighter in her crevasse of the sofa so that I would know she meant it. "No, Kecia, you are really beautiful."

That made me stop mid stitch, needle in between my fingers halfway thought the seam of my project. I froze and looked at her, my eyes danced on a tear drop. I had to check if she could see me from where I sat. I had to make sure she was talking to me even when there was no one else in the room. "Really?" Was all I could say when I gazed in her eyes, that were so confident. I had never heard that before. Not even from my parents. Whom, incidentally spent most of

their time buying me the next diet craze
instead of paying attention to the fact that
I hardly, ate or slept, or that every
morning I would heave my insides into a
trashcan. No, matter how much they
loved me they never paid that much
attention. They chalked all my issue down
to being fat. And so did I until I heard my
great grandmother say, "Kecia, you are
really beautiful."

She could tell I was struggling with
the news. My stuttered *really*, hung in the
air as if it was dangling from tattered
rope. But she shook her head unwavering
and said "Yes really suga, and don't you
every forget it. You hear?"

"Yes, Grandma Lynch." I said, trying my hardest not to sound shaken but I was.

And with that, it was over, she went back to watching her soaps and I went back to sewing. It was like we never spoke a word but the mood in the room had changed, I had changed. That night I cried. I cried because with all the things that were happening in my life something so simple, so easy to say 'you are beautiful' had changed me. I felt like a gift had been given to me that day. Somebody that loved me had told me I was beautiful.

Now when I think of my great grandmother I think of that day and when I look in the mirror I say "Kecia, you're really beautiful," with a smile. I wonder if she knew she saved my life that day just by say something so simple and true.

One Dozen Broken Eggs = 12
Broken Hearts

I imagine that broken hearts resemble cracked eggs, jagged crushed shell, and soupy love interior spilling out all over the place. Then it makes me wonder, "How many people are walking around with yoke dripping all over their shoes?"

I am in constant
guilt
of wanting things
I cannot
and will never
have

The Things Stars are Made Of

The elusion
of love
only exist on
Earth
for out
in the vastness
of space
you pray only
for
love's illusion
to brighten
the
empty reaches
of loneliness
your new
unreachable star

Class Is In Session

I have never been one for studying. I have never been one for purposely reading the same piece of text over and over for the sake of regurgitating it to pass a test or some class that I am twenty years too advanced to bother with. Then there is him, hair cropped neat at his ears, black as shoe polish. Eyes that tell stories of past lives and lost hopes muddy brown but shining amber in the sun. That same sun that cast an angelic glow on his medium build muscular frame, soft from never knowing the inside of a gym. He walked in and I found myself...I won't say studying, but I will say observing the careless way in which he tousled his hair as he spoke to everyone but me. I noticed him strut chest out, head high, doing his best impression of a peacock. I was informed – looking him dead in the eye- that he loves rainy days as much as I do. Although, I may not study, I am learning him in the off chance that one day I will be tested on my knowledge.

Walk Home

The moon light back-lit the trees
casting long creeping shadows
along the ground

Long skinny finger branches
tickled concrete cracks
and the weary side of soles

Along that adumbrate road
Under serpentine wooden knuckles
First love did bloom

With nervous looks
and fumbling tongues
Two hearts did confess their love

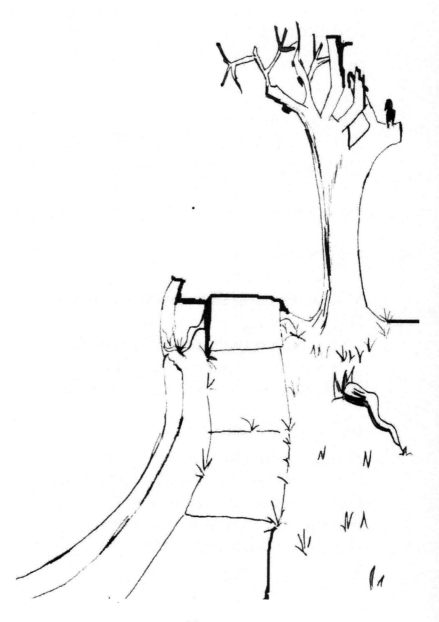

33

The Story of Us

I.

We spoke in poetry
Our eyes locked on melodic phrases
That told me what We should be
But, we didn't act on them
Nether one of us took that step,
                              the faithful
leap to leave the
Friend zone behind, Scared?
Maybe our long stares were too intense
Our life giving conversations
That watered the ground, too fertile
Our maybe we just did not know
A step was required to move us forward

We had everything
A swift friendship
Full of playful prose and laughing fits
I was invisibly drawn to you
An unspoken bond stronger than
We had anticipated
Please, say you felt it?

Because I felt it
It was as if I was earth and you my moon,

or you were the Sun
And I am every other planet fighting
For a change to be blessed with your light

Without ever having to dive to deep
Forcing the words to the surface
They were there dancing to the rhythm of
our beat
And you careened with me
Gliding, shifting and shaking
Past what eyes could see

You had become a part of me,
        and I a part of you
The purple to your red and blue
Combination of emotions
Identical vocal symmetry
Our tongues did magic
While we watched in awe
Rhyme fell from our being
Peeling away our natural aversions to love

We became new beings
Trusting in one another
Seeing past faults
Sending well wishes
And unseen kisses
We spoke in poetry

II.

Poetry left unspoken
Festers and dies
That is what you told me once
Or maybe that is some unscrupulous
Concoction of my making
I don't remember
I don't remember where
My begin began and yours ended
All I know is that
I have been cut in half
Severed by your act of simply
Moving away and forgetting to call
I wish that this poetry
That I want to whisper
Into your ear would fester
Shrivel up like how I feel inside
and die; turn to dust and blow far away
from here
What was that next step we where to take
We don't know
We never did
All I know is that this
Sensation kills

Only being able to see your face in
memories
Or pictures we took
Is another shot to the gut
No, its not a fatal wound
Just one that bleeds leisurely
There is a trail behind me
Marking all the places I have been
searching to see if that magic was not
Ours but theirs
And now my stomach is digesting those
bullets as well.
I regret ever sharing my happy song
Because now it holds a gun to my head

And I don't want to die yet
So it's banned from my musical library
I thought we were happy
Dancing to invisible songs in the key of
love
Finishing each other sentences
Speaking in poetry.
Floating on the ebb and flow of us
Because my heart tells me there is more
More prose to be made

More music to be bobbed to
More secret sessions of rhythmic love
making
To the sound of our hearts
Beating to the same cadence
The fast friendship that bloomed between
us
Has been cut and left to die
Pretty in a bowl
And I am not mad about it
I just wish this feeling of being halved
Of missing the whole I used to be a part of
Did not exist

III.

It's funny how life goes.
How we once loved
    so swift and naive
    believing that you were the puzzle
    piece
    missing from my life
    making me whole when we found
We spoke the same broken language
Just fragmented clicks and half
pronounced syllables
But to my ears it sounded like poetry
    a mystical love song
    that had me so bound to you
    I was forcing us to be one
I can only speak for myself
When I say I am glad that you fled
    because we were prisoners to
chemical reaction.
That was not love.
That was lust in the most broken down of
definitions
    a tragic Shakespearian play
    destined to die in the end

you my Emo Romeo
traveling my thoughts in your
black skinnies
me, your Diva Juliet
proclaiming our love in dramatic
fashion
'Cause I needs my audience.
While I was performing for the crowd
You where learning,
    watching us drive faster toward a
    brick wall.
Smart, you found a way out
    severed all ties because you could
    see
    how toxic we were,
    and I would have only sucked you
    back in
    with my charm and that chemical
    compound
    thundering under our skin.

There was something there,
    and if we where different people
    maybe,

maybe we could have lasted a
lifetime.
You and me, were us
     too young to know how love
     worked
     too infatuated to care
     holding on to the fantasy
     that love would find a way.
But love never does.
It must be directed
     and we never would have
     we would have frozen, doomed
     like a opossum in the middle of a
     highway
     waiting for the other one to take the
     lead
I am not bitter
I am older, wiser, smarter
I see the flaws of the past
I am hopeful
I am willing to try again
If you are still willing to love me

Vantage Point

My ties to you are
strenuous at best
held together by
Weak staples
And stretched out rubber bands
I am always falling away
but you find me
And staple me back in place
I wonder why?

I wonder why
you never tell me
to hold on to your
Coat sleeves or
your ankles?
Why you never
fling me around
your neck or
waist for a better grip?

You hold on to me,
While I struggle for
Breath like I've
been climbing this
Mountain under
my own power,
You hold on to me
with pink strained fingers
while I cry about
what couldn't be.

Yet you climb,
One foot in front of
The other, one hand
To grab the rock face
Of the mountain
One hand to keep me
Just let me fall
I beg, face burning
with tears and indifference
Why don't you just let me fall?

You don't answer me
You climb higher and higher
While I cry, why.
And then you say
it sure and strong,
no note out of place,
not a hint of struggle
in your voice
*Because we haven't reached
the top yet. You have got
to see the world from there.*

I Don't Know What Love Is

I don't know what love is.

I guess that is evident
in the way I write

About lips
pressed together seamlessly

Or about hands
clutching muscles mercilessly

or about eyes
catching first looks passionately

I don't know what love is
anymore than I know
where the wind starts and stops

I just know
that this feeling
this dull ache in my chest
eager muscles locked in embrace
wont dissipate, wont go away

It could be anything
but until I am sure
I am going to call
it what I hope it could be
I'm going to call it Love

These are things that have never happened, but if the thread that holds the fabric of dreams together were the same thread that stitched together reality, then they would have.

You kissed me
Long, soft.
Your lips
Against my lips
Your hands
Squeezing at the
Skin on my hips
My arms around
Your neck clinging
There for life
To be transferred
The act of
Mouth to mouth resuscitation
You kissed me
Long, soft
Hard, teeth and tongue
Fiery melting into one glob
Passion clawing at hearts

You let me in
I let you in
Under the misty night
Sky, stars drowned out
By city lights
You kissed me
I kissed you
And it was perfect.

Superlative Amour Argot

Drape your thousand word
love letter, stuffed with five
syllable colloquy, over
the brittle bone of my shoulders.
Paint your regalia on my breast
make me super human
through the strength of your tongue.

Earth song

The honey bee
chases nectar
from flower
to flower
The drummer
follows notes
with sticks
banging in key
Life dances
on rhythms
of heartbeats
We breathe
inhale exhale
consonance melody
lovers symphony

I stopped searching for
the hidden meaning in your words
Stopped trying to decipher
Between the lies you tell me
And the lies I tell myself
I don't care anymore

53

Realistically Speaking

I was told to be realistic,
by a cousin one evening while watching
"Just Wright"
She said "How many women that size end
up with a man like that?"
I said "Honestly I don't know, that's not
something I keep up with."
And I don't
But now sitting here, alone
I hear the things she implied
The things the world implies with the
"truth"

Daily I get fed the facts
The truth of obesity
"the curse of being a fat girl in a skinny
society"
Belly fat leads to Heart Attacks
Being fat shaves years off your life
I could go on but why,
We get the point

Facts don't always equate the truth

These are one sided facts
I believe the world of skinny hears
Fat is ugly
Fat is disgusting
I glad I am not fat
While they suck down their five dollar
double shot lattes

But those of us that happen to be Fat
Those that live in our fatty skin everyday
Hear
Because you are fat you do not deserve
Love
Acceptance
To be heard

See the fundamental problem with saying
something is bad
Is that we never get to what is good about
it
Don't get me wrong the medical facts of
being fat are
Just that Facts

But truth is the way fat people are
perceived and treated
Along with how we feel

I have heard less
that I deserve
the happiness I seek
than the facts
that happens to be me

Unfortunately
I am not afraid
to love the fatty
Skin that
this
beautiful girl
happens to come in
and if you rather
remind me of "facts"
than embrace
the truth
then honestly I have no time for you

My skin is not sin

The skin that I am in leads me to be
persecuted
With out reason to hold me at gun point
This wonderfully dark pigment
Covering my muscles and bone holding
all of me in
The mother of all skin tones begins with
this
Skin
Are you jealous?
Because my skin can do something that
your skin can't.
Is it jealousy because my skin can take the
vitamin d from the sun
And produce a color so beautiful
Hold the sun captive like a flower
Blooming golden nutty tones in my petals
This skin that I live in is not sin
It does magic
It can birth a rainbow of colors
But you wouldn't know that
Because you persecute me for
My skin

And I love my skin
This cream chocolate coating of cells
This blissful home for my soul
The thing that I am is posted on my face
My Arms, my legs, my back, my belly
My skin is not sin
Nor do you have the right to treat me like
it is
Because you see your skin as superior
Let me give you a basic color lesson
White is the absence of all color
Black is all color blended
So your fair complexion
Resides somewhere inside of me

Blank Wall

I am staring at a blank wall.
Void of interest in any way.
But I can't seem to turn away
I am stuck.

Mesmerized by the blank
Captivated by absence
I wonder
How could I lose interest in you?

Surely you are more
Riddled with bullet points
Showing me the way
To your wonders

But I don't see them
You are featureless
A blank wall
White with all your absence

But at least on the wall I
Cant turn away from
I can hang a picture
Of my interesting self

Just Because I Was A Little Ghetto Kid Doesn't Mean I Wanted To Be A Rapper

Part One

Just because I was a little ghetto kid
doesn't mean I wanted to be a rapper
bopping my head to rap music
Stealing their lyrics
spilling them like poetry
when the songs ended
tapping those
deep bass-y beats into
our dinted marble linoleum kitchen table
While momma in curlers
Lectured me
On the importance of an education
Long red nails click- clacking to her
speech
Momma preached
the sky is the limit
Momma was music to me
everything about her

stretched past where my eyes could see
nowhere to everywhere
I listened
She didn't want me to grow up
Like those fools out in the street
destined to die young or live a life in jail
 While we lived our life behind bars
I thought it ironic that I should
have dreams that soared
when I couldn't see the trees
outside the kitchen window past
the frilly ironwork that was supposed
to keep criminals out
I only felt like we were being kept in
trained, conditioned
to a life that was mine to live

No more than this,
Whatever dream I have
would have to fit inside the cage that I
lived
But
Just because I was a little ghetto kid
doesn't mean I wanted to be a rapper

Part Two

Just because I was a little ghetto kid
doesn't mean I was not interested in
The cultures of the world
even though I was limited
to the block
and street light time scales
I was in before dark
safe from the shadows
creeping along the sidewalk
with boney fingers and fat joint
Hoping to take me under their wing
Inside is were I dreamed of
being high above the clouds
Transported all over the world
Learning, and growing
Just because I was a little ghetto kid
Doesn't mean that I wasn't aware
that because of the color of my skin
A lot of people and places in the world
wouldn't want me
But I wont waste tears on things that don't
want me
I won't let my block

Geography or
Ignorance limit me
I will rise above it all
Just because I was a little ghetto kid
Doesn't mean I wanted to be a rapper

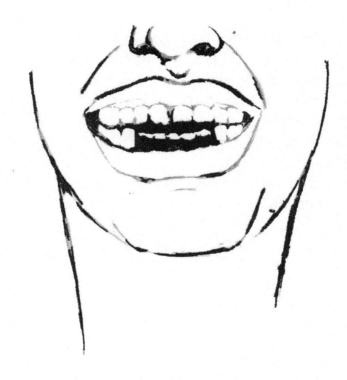

Part Three

Just because I was a little ghetto kid
doesn't mean that I am Worth less
Than anyone one else
And I never wanted to be a rapper
But the lines
in these verses
spit like lyrics
Frilly ironworks of rhythm
Hell there are worst things
To be

Interest Rate of 96%

I stand head bowed
Muscles tensed for the judgment
Of closed eyes
When I speak the truth
Ripping the sonorous parlance
still dripping with ichor
From my vibrating voice box
Yet they expatiate
Lies as thin as
One-ply tissue paper
And the sheep listen
Buoyantly walking
Into to the gullet of the wolves
Selling you your freedom
For the price of bondage
I bare not the mark of martyr
Therefore the freedom I preach
is deemed mad
preposterous hallucinations
of the wicked
I find it laughable
When they see with closed eyes

and sit in thralldom draped in heavy
chains
bartering your children's liberty
for the price of designer ordure

Self-reflection of Imperfection

We project
Our mind is made that way
reading only partial truths
broken phrases
choked off sentences
we fill in the blanks
listening to
Invisible speakers
Figments of imagination
Warping what we
Perceive
You don't see me
I am merely
A reflection of a
hidden part of you
you can't understand
what I say
It's over powered
but the thumping
of your own heart
The metronome
of constant self-reflection

Self – hatred
Self…
Love
If it was love
Our projections
would please us
and we would
Be happy
But that's not the case
In the matter
we dislike
What we perceive
Because we hate
Self
And we see Self
We project

The Sun

She has managed
to fold me
crease my waist
curl my body
curve my will

She had managed
to fold me
bend my cast iron heart
Soften the hard welded edge
warm the cold stagnate blood

She has managed
to fold me
and in shifting my position
she has brought me
into the light

Don't Be So Magnanimous

Stoic you trudge through
the thickets of thorny bushes
and dagger tongues
to be rewarded with nothing
Empty thanks toasted
to cheap wine and stale bread
But you march on
Diligent in your journey
Whatever your destination
hurtles do not phase you
you want not glory
just the end of this season
of uncontrollable numbness
Its been so cold you lost
most of your toes to frostbite
But you will not freeze
Slogging threw shit as
high as your ankles you can't
be stopped, and no one would
dare dream of it

You should know
That with all the abuse you
take you don't
have to fair it alone
Here is my should to lean on

I left the battered
navy blue and
bruised purples
of yesterday behind
with the closing
of my midnight eyes
To dream

To You who watches over me,

Dear You,
I held your gaze for hours,
glowing dusty rose
against a navy blue blanket
eaten through by thousands of moths.
You sat there
understanding, absorbing
every word that pasted my lips
every hope, every wish.
I wanted to embrace you
but you are always too far away to touch.
So I sang you my love.
Thank you for always
being there when I need you most.

Your Dear Friend

The End in A or Maybe...

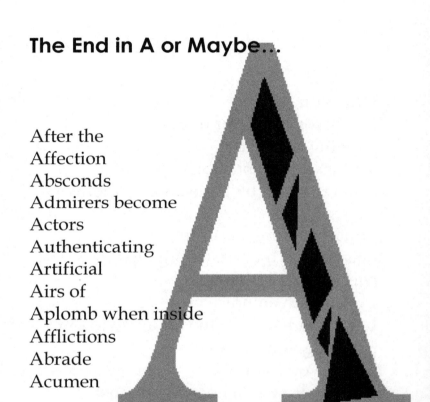

After the
Affection
Absconds
Admirers become
Actors
Authenticating
Artificial
Airs of
Aplomb when inside
Afflictions
Abrade
Acumen

The Beginning

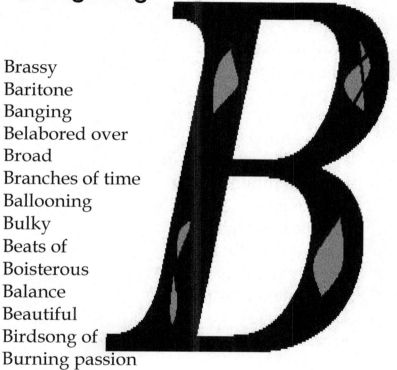

Brassy
Baritone
Banging
Belabored over
Broad
Branches of time
Ballooning
Bulky
Beats of
Boisterous
Balance
Beautiful
Birdsong of
Burning passion

Of The Relationship From C to Z

Convivial caresses
Diligent desire
Effortless
Fervent
Gallivanting
Hyperactively **without**
Incubus **innervations**
Just Jovial
Kinetic ecstasy
Lackadaisically loving
Merrily maneuvered
Neophyte of history
Oblivious to
Precarious
Questions Quelling
Repose to
Serendipitous sentiments
Tactically

Ushering in
Vexation
With weathered
Xysters
Yielding
Zealous yearning for death

Lips Aflame

He struck a match. Cupped his hands over the flame, then engulfed the filtered tip of his cigarette. He sucked in two long pulls before shaking out the match into the air leaving a fading streak of gray in the dark of her bedroom. He touched the still smoking match to his tongue before flicking it onto her bedroom floor. It was his practice after sex. One cigarette, one match flung upon the carpet.

She didn't understand this ritual of his. At first she thought he was trying to see if he could start a fire while she lay in bed, head swimming, watching. His fingers curled holding the match and cigarette, elbows bend and elongate, muscle contract and relax, she lay there watching it all and waiting for everything to rest upon his lips. She could stare at those things for hours. She knew the contours of his mouth by heart, fingers, and tongue. She could pick his mouth out of a line up without him ever speaking a word. This was her favorite part of the evening, even more than his hands exploring her body. She liked watching him smoke naked head against headboard, Adam's apple bobbing on the sea of his throat, spitting his plum into the dark air.

Passing Thought

I had some inspiration
some little tidbits of sunshine
information to enlighten
crashing adjectives and adverbs
over flowing with meaning
metaphor and simile abound
but I hesitated to
place nouns on paper
subjects were lost
verbs misplaced
curious whispers in the wind

Ugly Duckling

She is not pretty
her teeth are chipped
her hair is dry and stringy
her eyes are dull
her body is dented, hard, lumpy
and her voice, that voice
compared to her every other girls
voice pours out golden honey
but
her heart is pure
that is what makes her so lovely
and every night before I close my eyes
I say thank you
because that beautiful girl loves me

Fraction Of Time

It was the thump....thump
that millisecond
Pause
The needed rest to gear
The heart up for
It's next beat.
The place were the
Electrical charge stays
Buzzing
Like deadly fences
Or stinging bees.
In that infinitesimal
Faction of a second
Our eyes meet
And you managed
To hook your
Power supply to
My cold dead heart
and
shock me
alive

Awake
Had I been
In deep slumber
Like sleeping beauty
Or
Had I been walking
Looking everywhere
Else
But ahead?
Now,
I see you
Shrouded in angelic light
I never believed in love at first sight
But damn
I'm stuck
Caught hook line and sinker
To your invisible string
Reel me in
Drop me in a glass bowl
And keep me as a pet for life.
I will eat
The scraps that fall
From your waiting lips
Like kisses.
Just hold on to me tight
Never let your

Hands fall from
My hips
Or my breath will slow.
In this marathon
of hearts ownership
You wouldn't want to
be to slow.
No,
you couldn't be.
You're a Bandit in black
Sticky fingered,
Kleptomaniac.
You stole from me
In a millisecond
A fraction
of a
fraction of time
You had me resting
in the palm of your hands
Bating eyes
and blushing
wishing
that you
were mine.

Two Birds

Part One

It was two of them. One old, and one young enough to still be considered young. Just the two of these birds slouched in leather bucket seats. One was always sitting behind the wheel of the massive Buick steam rolling down the highway. The young one watched the old one drive first. It was a pantomime in driving really. It seemed so far away from the actual act of driving, hands at ten and two, shaking the wheel back and fourth in quick successions. *People don't really drive like that* the young one thought as she watched with her very own eyes as a truth she held was proven false. That was part of the appeal of watching the old birds talons curve dark around the vanilla cream of the steering wheel cover. It was like watching a World Record be broken, kind of amazing, kind of saddening, and completely unable to turn away from.

The old one sighed. She reached deep into her lungs and pulled out words covered in worry and stress. In those words she carried the wrinkles of being a mother and a grandmother and a life walked this Earth, she carried wisdom and she also carried questions searching for wisdom. The young one listened to the way her heart broke when she spoke of the reasons for their road trip. The young swallowed it all, drank in her heartbreak, her worries and wisdom, she swallowed down her strife and her past. She didn't mind, that is what this was after all, a transfer of memories, of power, of life. The time huddled together in the leather interior of a vehicle that once belonged to a newly deceased person was all about passing something down, so it could live on in the life of someone young with meaning. Morals spoken like fables and stored like fairy tales to be recited at the bedsides of chicks, golden new feathers still soft and impressionable taking in every word with eager ears.

"I just don't know what he was thinking. I mean really, I just don't get it." She sighed, talons at ten and two. "That's my son, but I just don't get it."

"What is there to get...that's just who he is. But you know that." The young one a Sparrow, sang out the only answer she knew to be true and not speculation, before turning her head to watch the landscape of a rising sun on a desert plain awake with a ruby twinkle that burn her eyes.

"You're right." The old crow said with a sigh and wrinkles and talons at ten and two. "You're right."

Part Two

The young bird, a Sparrow was right
about a lot of things. She was right about a
lot of things because she never tried to
find the answers. She would just let the
truth float out there. Sparrows don't
answer questions. They sing lovely tunes
that state truths, in lovely melodies that
make you forget the question. But the
young Sparrow, mind full of wander, and
head full of melodious phrases,
understood that the answer is not always
that important, but beauty is paramount.
Even in the disaster of a situation this
drive exploded from, a song crept up into

the hollow cavity of her scarred lungs and
caressed the lumpy tissue. She held it tight
as the old Crow, deep dark talons at ten
and two, sighed and thought, and
worried, with glassy eyes.

The old Crow cawed, and creaked as she
pressed her foot into the floor of the car,
filing away her worries with each mile
East she put behind them. Each mile she
filed in order, Love of family, the hurt that
family causes, the hurt she causes to her
family, and the incident. She files them all
away carefully knowing that sometimes
love looks like hurt and hurt looks like
love and how they all molded together to
explode in your face while you wear your
best...*Armageddon*, for a family of birds, all

different kinds, that flock together in a
sharp V, under normal circumstances. She
filed it all away, mile by mile, with sighs
as her shoulders got tighter, talons at ten
and two, glassy eyed and winkled.
The Sparrow watched and listened, turned
the discomfort of the Crow into songs in
her head. She bobbed to the sounds of
filing, and tires, and road running
backwards, and sighing, and cawing, and
creaking mechanical joints. It was lovely
music, the cacophony of different sounds
banging together. She like the sound of
explosions and the shattering glass sound
hearts make when they break, because
that meant she was growing, and living,
and building stories to pass down, or

simply stories to re-tale to a spongy mind as a tales of triumph, heroism. The songs came, touched lightly the scared tissue of her lungs, beautifully she held them on her breath. Not ready for them to escape her beak just yet, so she listened, built melodies in her head out of filing, and cawing, and talons, and tires, and road, and explosions. It's all quite lovely music in a young Sparrows ears.

Part Three

"What are you thinking about?" The Old Crow asked the Sparrow, whose eyes were searching the flat landscape. "Breakfast," The Sparrow said absentmindedly, when really she was just listening, quietly listening to the Crow's caw, metal joint shift, glass shatter, and slamming metal filing cabinet doors. "I could go for some waffles." The Old Crow declared, rather lively. In fact it was rather far away from her early disposition. The Sparrow made note. "I tell you what, the next IHOP we see we'll get breakfast."

"Okay, that works." The sparrow agreed never removing her eyes from the flat desert landscape of California that blended seamlessly into Arizona.

The sparrow thought to herself how funny it was that the cacti looked like little prickly people doing a no rain dance out in the middle of nowhere. It made her laugh to think such an outrageous thought dancing plants. The silliness of the idea that had popped into her bird brain did not stop it from mesmerizing her. It stole so much of her attention in fact that she would miss the next five signs pointing the way to IHOP.

Well into the normally blistering city of Phoenix, Arizona the two birds, the

Sparrow and the Old Crow sat in an IHOP. The Old Crow, with her talons and metal joints sawed happily at her huge waffle while the Sparrow, all bird brained and nonsensical pecked at her veggie filled omelet and soupy fruit bowl.

"I'll drive when we leave here. I got the address to the Robin's place. Six hours away and then we will be half way to Houston." The Sparrow said sliding the last piece of her omelet down her beak.

"I could use the rest, my shoulder hurts." The Sparrow thought of the pantomime of driving. "I think it was from the other night." The Old Crow laughed half heartedly remembering Armageddon. "I just don't get it."

The Sparrow smiled, looked half-heartedly out the window. She wished she could shoulder some of the weight for the Crow but it seems her happy brainless state was positioned right on top of quicksand. Not quicksand of her own, but the quicksand of trying to shoulder others burdens. Sparrows packed light and were not much for carrying baggage with them, their light hearts wouldn't allow it.

"I have to use the bathroom before we go." The Sparrow announced. She popped out of her seat shook off the heavy feeling that had started to push her into the sand and flittered off into the restroom gracefully like only Sparrows do.

Part Four

The two birds, the Old Crow with her
glassy eyes and slamming file cabinets,
and talons, and metal limbs, and the
young Sparrow with her singing and light
heartedness pulled into the snow covered
city of Las Cruces, New Mexico. Lost at
first, sent on a minor detour by the
computed voice of Jill (the Sparrow decide
the GPS as all things helpful needed a
proper name) but soon guided in by the
Red breast of the beautiful young Robin
covered in layer upon layer of warmth.
Once out on the icy path way to the den of

the Robin, the Sparrow took note of the sound that ice made as it crunched under her boots. The Sparrow liked the new sound as it made a new music in her ears that she begin to hum along with.

"Be careful." The Old Crow cawed at the Sparrow who was prone to spilling herself all over concrete.

"Ha! I was just about to tell you the same thing." The Sparrow laughed as she carefully crunched on top of more of the icy walkway and up the ice covered stairs.

"Both of you be careful," giggled the Robin from behind the two birds. "I'm the apartment on the right." The Robin pointed out the way from behind them. "The door is open."

The Sparrow was the first through the door. She had not realized how quickly the cold had seeped through her plumage and nestled into her bones. The warmth of the Robin's lightly cluttered den felt like dragons breath on her frozen Sparrow cheeks. She was pleased to meet the heat from the invisible dragon. She even heard the Crows metal limbs relax into the heat when she crossed the threshold.

"It's very cute in here," the Old Crow cawed as she shrugged out of her coat. "Thank you!" The Robin chirped. "Oh, and I made you two dinner." The Robin said fluffing the vibrant feathers of her breast while filling her lungs with warm air.

The Sparrow dropped her coat and bag in the nearest available seat before wondering through the Robin's apartment to the kitchen. On the stove the Sparrow found the dinner (in all of its vibrant colors) the Robin made.

"I don't have a microwave but I'll just reheat everything on the stove really quickly for you." The Robin said from behind the Sparrow.

"This looks really good." The Sparrow chirped, happy to see the meal because salty road food did not agree with her delicate digestive tract.

The Robin turned on the stove to warm the nourishment and offered her guest a beer. Both the Sparrow and the Old Crow happily accepted the libations. After good drinks and good food they all (the old Crow, the Sparrow, and the Robin) relaxed into the evening with ease, while light conversation floated through the air.

Part Five

The Sparrow and the Robin stirred gently
before the sun rose into the frost bitten air.
They chirped and giggled into winter
clothes and boots, fluttered about the
Robin's warm apartment until they were
ready to greet the frozen air that hugged
the desert floor.

They chipped the snow and ice off the
window of the car as they shared
pleasantries about the time that had past
since their last meeting and their hopes for
the future. The Old Crow rested. The
chatter continued as they drove to the
store so The Sparrow could stock up on
road snacks. They didn't stop the pleasant

squawking until The Sparrow and Old Crow were pulling away from the curb to continue their journey down interstate 10. The Old Crow with her creaking limbs and filing drawers sat quietly reserved in the passenger seat as the sparrow silently filled with glee and new music drove them across the Texas state border.

As the road melted away being them so did the ice as the flat Texas terrain stretched on for miles. There was a fuel stop and a place swap, and loose lug nut on the rear driver side tire. The rest of the trip passed away just as the scenery of the landscape was born in front of them and died when it was out of view.

There was talking, but nothing
meaningful enough to remember. The
Crow signed, the Sparrow sang interesting
lullabies in her head and along with the
radio whether she knew the words or not.
The highway curved away behind them in
an asphalt river dotted with yellow
flowers. The sun moved across the sky,
sunrise to sunset.

Part Six

Once at the nest of the Skylark, and a
vibrant family, The Old Crow and
Sparrow rested their weary feathers. Both
found time to wash the dust of the
highway down the drain in a swirl of hot
water and soap before they laid down for
bed on the leather sofas The Skylark had
in her living room. In the morning, the
Sparrow full of song and the Old Crow
with talons at ten and two parted ways.
For the Crow home was six hours east
down highway, and winding roads lined
with thousands of trees. For the Sparrow,
there was one more night in Texas. One
last night on the road that was full of loud

rooms boasting of music, lined in flavored smoke, spilling over with alcohol, and happiness. But in the morning after the Sparrow would have to leave the Skylark and her family to fly back home. The end of the Sparrows journey was where it all began.

What if? And Flowers

For Aiyana Jones

What if we lived on a flower?
Drove crimson petal streets
drank the sticky sweet nectar
Of gold soaked rivers
Slumbered in endless
corridors of green
sparkled like hazy dreams
fading fast from the waking mind
I would still love you
with a same intensity
the sun erupts into everyday.

What if I were a flower,
and the only way of expression
was bloom, then sun, then death?
I would bloom for you
stretch my Technicolor
limbs to the sky
devour Aurora's tears
then turn morose, sickly
creased with brown and faded hue

refuse to be, refuse to take nourishment
from Adam's ale and die.
That would mean I love you
If *I* was a flower and that was my only
expression to make, I'd make it for you.

Epilogue

As we reach the end of this journey, this book, this whatever, this is... I have no more clarity than I had. But even without clarity I feel better for having shared it. These poems, prose, and short stories are bite size bits of me that are now yours for your consumption. Some highly fiction, some bitter truths, some are sweet and easy to swallow, and some you have to chew. They are part of my journey that I feel uncomfortable enough to share with you.

Thank you. May we travel together again
soon.

Printed in Great Britain
by Amazon

38523317R00066